202579

THE FIRST MOON LANDING

STORY:
ELIZABETH HUDSON-GOFF AND DALE ANDERSON

ILLUSTRATIONS:
GUUS FLOOR, ALEX CAMPBELL, AND ANTHONY SPAY

WORLD ALMANAC® LIBRARY

FOR MANY YEARS, THE UNITED STATES AND THE SOVIET UNION WERE LOCKED IN A POWER STRUGGLE. BOTH POWERS WANTED TO LEAD THE WORLD IN SCIENCE AND TECHNOLOGY. BOTH WANTED TO BE THE FIRST TO PUT A MAN ON THE MOON.

IN OCTOBER 1957, THE SOVIET UNION SHOCKED THE REST OF THE WORLD WHEN THEY LAUNCHED SPUTNIK. SPUTNIK WAS THE FIRST ARTIFICIAL SATELLITE TO ORBIT EARTH.

ONE MONTH LATER, THE SOVIET UNION SENT A DOG INTO SPACE ON SPUTNIK 2. THIS FLIGHT PROVED THAT A LIVING THING COULD SURVIVE A TRIP TO SPACE.

YURI GAGARIN FROM THE SOVIET UNION WAS THE FIRST HUMAN TO TRAVEL IN SPACE. ON APRIL 12, 1961, HE COMPLETED ONE ORBIT AROUND EARTH.

BUT THE UNITED STATES WAS CATCHING UP. ON MAY 5, 1961, ALAN SHEPARD BECAME THE FIRST AMERICAN IN SPACE.

IN 1962, JOHN GLENN BECAME THE FIRST AMERICAN TO ORBIT EARTH. VIEWS OF THE LAND AND OCEANS OF EARTH FILLED HIS WINDOW. AS HE CIRCLED THE PLANET, HE WATCHED FOUR SUNSETS.

WHEN GLENN RETURNED, A HUGE PARADE WAS HELD IN NEW YORK CITY IN HIS HONOR. ABOUT 4 MILLION PEOPLE SHOWERED HIM WITH CHEERS AND TICKERTAPE. WITH GLENN'S FLIGHT, THE UNITED STATES HAD TAKEN A GIANT STEP TOWARD REACHING THE MOON!

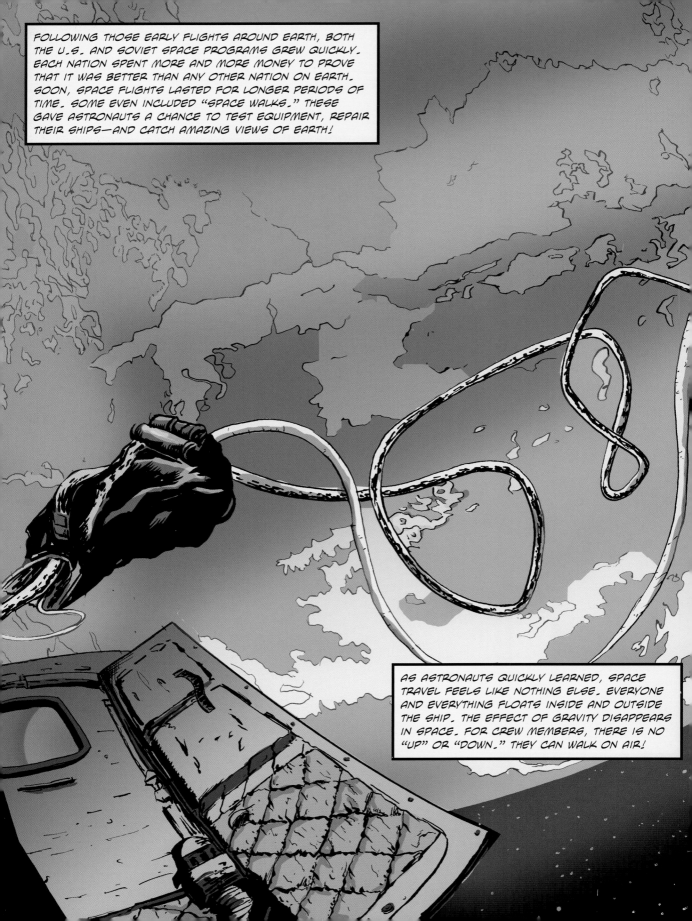

FOLLOWING THOSE EARLY FLIGHTS AROUND EARTH, BOTH THE U.S. AND SOVIET SPACE PROGRAMS GREW QUICKLY. EACH NATION SPENT MORE AND MORE MONEY TO PROVE THAT IT WAS BETTER THAN ANY OTHER NATION ON EARTH. SOON, SPACE FLIGHTS LASTED FOR LONGER PERIODS OF TIME. SOME EVEN INCLUDED "SPACE WALKS." THESE GAVE ASTRONAUTS A CHANCE TO TEST EQUIPMENT, REPAIR THEIR SHIPS—AND CATCH AMAZING VIEWS OF EARTH!

AS ASTRONAUTS QUICKLY LEARNED, SPACE TRAVEL FEELS LIKE NOTHING ELSE. EVERYONE AND EVERYTHING FLOATS INSIDE AND OUTSIDE THE SHIP. THE EFFECT OF GRAVITY DISAPPEARS IN SPACE. FOR CREW MEMBERS, THERE IS NO "UP" OR "DOWN." THEY CAN WALK ON AIR!

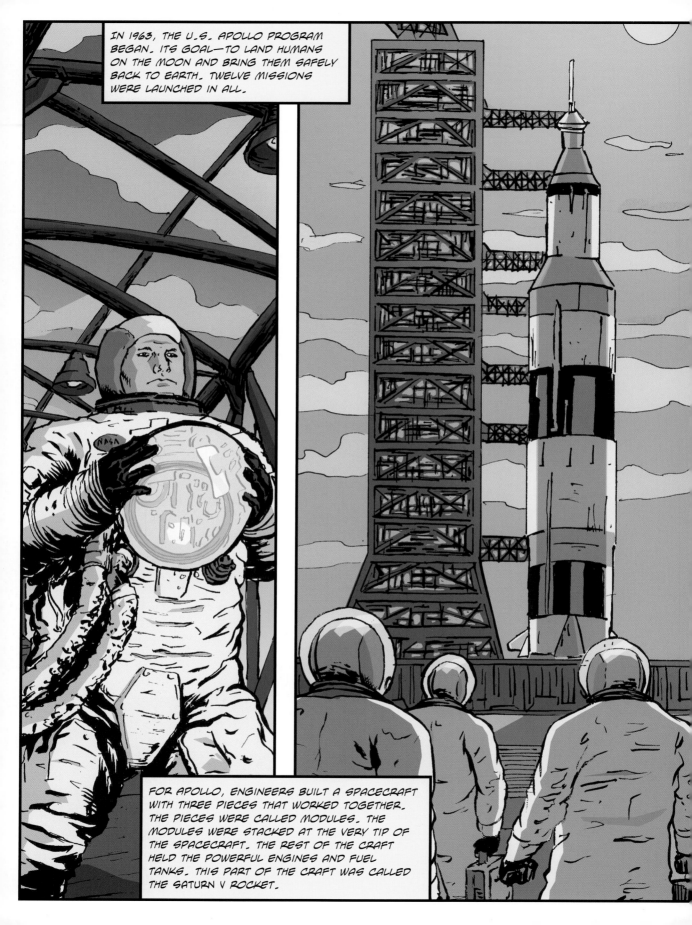

IN 1963, THE U.S. APOLLO PROGRAM BEGAN. ITS GOAL—TO LAND HUMANS ON THE MOON AND BRING THEM SAFELY BACK TO EARTH. TWELVE MISSIONS WERE LAUNCHED IN ALL.

FOR APOLLO, ENGINEERS BUILT A SPACECRAFT WITH THREE PIECES THAT WORKED TOGETHER. THE PIECES WERE CALLED MODULES. THE MODULES WERE STACKED AT THE VERY TIP OF THE SPACECRAFT. THE REST OF THE CRAFT HELD THE POWERFUL ENGINES AND FUEL TANKS. THIS PART OF THE CRAFT WAS CALLED THE SATURN V ROCKET.

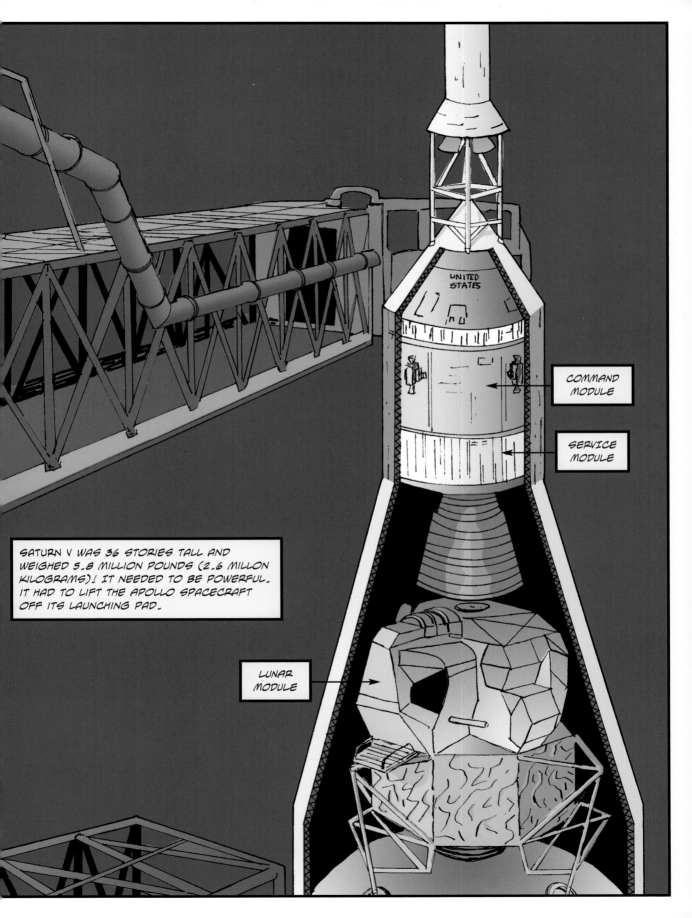

UNITED STATES

COMMAND MODULE

SERVICE MODULE

SATURN V WAS 36 STORIES TALL AND WEIGHED 5.8 MILLION POUNDS (2.6 MILLON KILOGRAMS)! IT NEEDED TO BE POWERFUL. IT HAD TO LIFT THE APOLLO SPACECRAFT OFF ITS LAUNCHING PAD.

LUNAR MODULE

SPACE MISSIONS WERE A TEAM EFFORT. THE ASTRONAUTS ON BOARD HAD DIFFERENT JOBS. MANY SCIENTISTS, ENGINEERS, DOCTORS AND FLIGHT EXPERTS WORKED ON THE GROUND.

INFORMATION WAS SENT TO AND FROM SPACE BY COMPUTERS. COMPUTERS WERE VERY NEW AND NOT VERY POWERFUL BY TODAY'S STANDARDS. BUT WITHOUT THEM, THE APOLLO PROGRAM WOULD NOT HAVE BEEN POSSIBLE.

TEN TEST FLIGHTS WERE LAUNCHED BEFORE THE FIRST MOONWALK. EVEN THE LUNAR MODULE MADE TEST LANDINGS ON EARTH. THESE TESTS HELPED SCIENTISTS AND ENGINEERS MAKE THE MOON LAUNCH AS SAFE AS POSSIBLE.

LIFTOFF!

IN A GIANT CLOUD OF SMOKE AND FIRE, APOLLO 11 LIFTED OFF INTO SPACE. DESTINATION—THE MOON!

AS LIFTOFF BEGAN, THE ASTRONAUTS LOOKED STRAIGHT INTO THE SKY. THE FIRST 15 SECONDS WERE ROUGH AND SCARY. THE ASTRONAUTS FELT EVERYTHING SHAKE WILDLY. THEN THE SKY GREW DARKER.

UP, UP, UP—THE PURE SPEED WAS ASTONISHING!

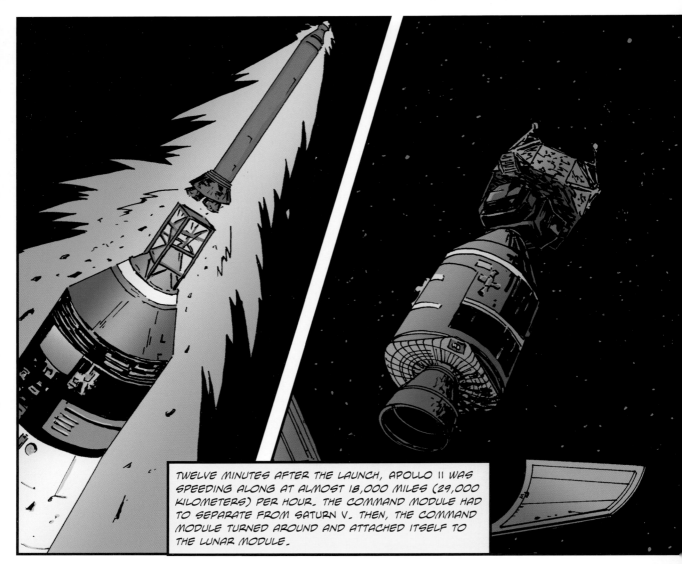

TWELVE MINUTES AFTER THE LAUNCH, APOLLO 11 WAS SPEEDING ALONG AT ALMOST 18,000 MILES (29,000 KILOMETERS) PER HOUR. THE COMMAND MODULE HAD TO SEPARATE FROM SATURN V. THEN, THE COMMAND MODULE TURNED AROUND AND ATTACHED ITSELF TO THE LUNAR MODULE.

THE ASTRONAUTS LIVED ON FREEZE-DRIED MEALS, SANDWICHES, AND DRINKS. IF A DRINK SPILLED, IT SPREAD IN BIG BUBBLES IN THE AIR. THEY COULD NOT SHOWER, AND THEIR "TOILETS" WERE SPECIAL PLASTIC BAGS. EVEN A SNEEZE ROSE IN THE AIR IN THE TINY BUBBLES. IN THEIR WEIGHTLESS ENVIRONMENT, THE THREE MEN MUST HAVE HAD SOME FUNNY MOMENTS ON THE WAY TO THE MOON.

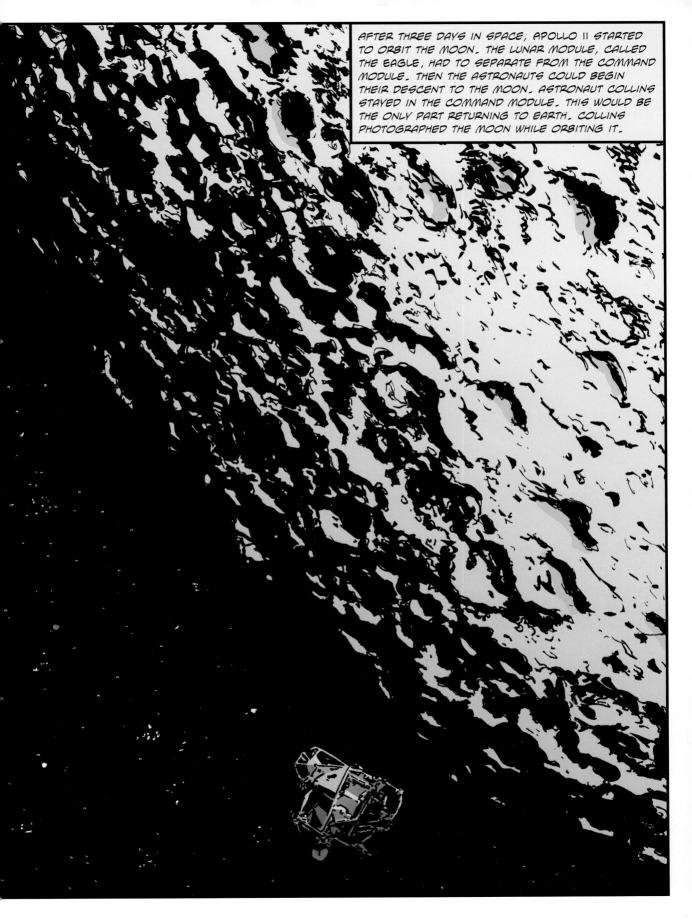

AFTER THREE DAYS IN SPACE, APOLLO 11 STARTED TO ORBIT THE MOON. THE LUNAR MODULE, CALLED THE EAGLE, HAD TO SEPARATE FROM THE COMMAND MODULE. THEN THE ASTRONAUTS COULD BEGIN THEIR DESCENT TO THE MOON. ASTRONAUT COLLINS STAYED IN THE COMMAND MODULE. THIS WOULD BE THE ONLY PART RETURNING TO EARTH. COLLINS PHOTOGRAPHED THE MOON WHILE ORBITING IT.

AS ALDRIN AND ARMSTRONG PREPARED TO LAND, THEY SAW DANGER BELOW. THE EAGLE WAS CLOSE TO THE GROUND AND HEADING FOR A CRATER FILLED WITH ROCKS!

ARMSTRONG MOVED THE LUNAR MODULE AWAY FROM THE CRATER. HE HAD SEVEN SECONDS OF LANDING FUEL LEFT. HE HAD TO FIND A PLACE TO LAND. ALL OF HIS YEARS OF TRAINING WERE NOW PUT TO THE TEST. WOULD THEY MAKE IT?

NEIL ARMSTRONG SLOWLY CLIMBED DOWN THE LADDER OF THE LUNAR LANDING MODULE AND STEPPED ON THE MOON'S SURFACE. HE COULD SEE THE BLUE-GREEN SPHERE OF EARTH FAR ABOVE HIM. HE COULD NOT HEAR THE CHEERS THAT ERUPTED FROM THERE.

BUZZ ALDRIN SOON JOINED ARMSTRONG. THE 2 MEN SPENT A TOTAL OF 21 HOURS ON THE MOON. THEY DID EXPERIMENTS AND TOOK PICTURES. THEY COLLECTED 46 POUNDS (21 KILOGRAMS) OF MOON ROCKS.

THEY PLANTED A U.S. FLAG.
THEY ALSO PUT UP A PLAQUE.

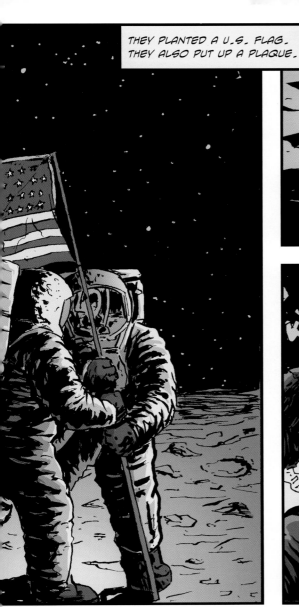

PRESIDENT RICHARD NIXON EVEN CALLED THEM ON THE TELEPHONE! THAT WAS A LONG DISTANCE CALL!

THE ASTRONAUTS' FOOTPRINTS ARE STILL THERE BECAUSE THERE IS NO RAIN OR WIND ON THE MOON.

IT WAS TIME TO RETURN TO EARTH.
MISSION CONTROL WAS NERVOUS. A
ROCKET HAD NEVER BEEN LAUNCHED
FROM ANYWHERE BESIDES EARTH
BEFORE.

EVERYONE SIGHED WITH RELIEF
WHEN THE ROCKETS FIRED UP.

THEN, THE TOP PART OF
THE LUNAR MODULE
SEPARATED FROM THE
BOTTOM PART. IT PUT
THE ASTRONAUTS BACK
INTO ORBIT AROUND
THE MOON. SUCCESS!

ONCE IN ORBIT, THE EAGLE DOCKED WITH THE COMMAND MODULE. ARMSTRONG AND ALDRIN REJOINED COLLINS.

THE EAGLE DROPPED INTO SPACE, TO FLOAT FREE, FOREVER. IT HAD DONE ITS JOB. THE COMMAND MODULE NOW HAD A NEW JOB TO DO—LEAVE LUNAR ORBIT AND BEGIN ITS JOURNEY BACK TO EARTH!

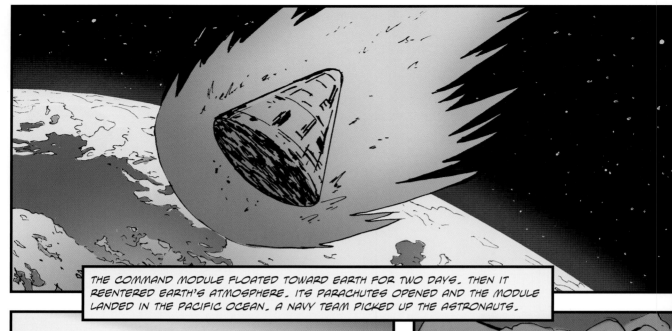

THE COMMAND MODULE FLOATED TOWARD EARTH FOR TWO DAYS. THEN IT REENTERED EARTH'S ATMOSPHERE. ITS PARACHUTES OPENED AND THE MODULE LANDED IN THE PACIFIC OCEAN. A NAVY TEAM PICKED UP THE ASTRONAUTS.

SPLASHDOWN!

NO ONE KNEW IF THE ASTRONAUTS BROUGHT BACK ANY DISEASES. SO THE THREE MEN HAD TO STAY AWAY FROM PEOPLE.

HORNET + 3

PRESIDENT NIXON VISITED THE ASTRONAUTS WHILE THEY LIVED IN A SEALED TRAILER.

AFTER THEY LEFT THE TRAILER, THE ASTRONAUTS WERE GREETED AS SUPERHEROES. THE WHOLE WORLD TALKED ABOUT APOLLO 11 AND ITS BRAVE CREW!

THE U.S. SPACE PROGRAM SENT FIVE MORE APOLLO MISSIONS TO THE MOON AFTER APOLLO 11. ASTRONAUTS COLLECTED MOON ROCKS AND METEORITES. THEY FOUND MINERALS ON THESE ROCKS THAT DID NOT EXIST ON EARTH. ONE OF THESE MINERALS WAS EVEN NAMED AFTER THE THREE APOLLO 11 ASTRONAUTS! THESE MISSIONS HELPED SCIENTISTS LEARN MORE ABOUT THE UNIVERSE AND PLANETS, INCLUDING EARTH.

OVER THE YEARS, THE U.S. SPACE PROGRAM GREATLY IMPROVED ITS EQUIPMENT. LATER APOLLO MISSIONS USED LUNAR ROVERS, OR MOON CARS, TO GET AROUND.

DURING THE 1970s, THE UNITED STATES AND THE SOVIET UNION BEGAN WORKING TOGETHER. BY 1975, A U.S. APOLLO SPACECRAFT HAD DOCKED IN SPACE WITH A SOVIET CRAFT.

THE TWO CREWS MET AND SHOOK HANDS. THEY CARRIED OUT EXPERIMENTS IN SPACE. THIS MEETING WAS ANOTHER GIANT STEP FOR MANKIND. THE WORLD WAS LEARNING TO WORK TOGETHER!

SPACE EXPLORATION CONTINUED AT ROCKET SPEED! DURING THE 1970s, THE U.S. SPACE PROGRAM HAD CREWS STUDY SPACE FROM A SPACE STATION CALLED SKYLAB. CREWS LIVED ON THE ORBITING STATION FOR MONTHS AT A TIME.

IN THE 1980s, THE U.S. PROGRAM BEGAN USING THE SPACE SHUTTLE FOR TRAVEL INTO SPACE. SPACE SHUTTLES CAN HOLD MORE ASTRONAUTS. THEY ALSO HAVE BETTER EQUIPMENT.

IN 1998, MANY COUNTRIES BEGAN WORK ON THE INTERNATIONAL SPACE STATION (ISS). THE ISS IS A HUGE LABORATORY AND LIVING SPACE. ONE OF THE THINGS THAT CREWS STUDY IS WAYS TO IMPROVE LIFE ON EARTH.

LAUNCHED INTO ORBIT IN 1990, THE HUBBLE SPACE TELESCOPE PROVIDES AMAZING INFORMATION ABOUT THE UNIVERSE. IT CAN SEE GALAXIES BILLIONS OF LIGHT YEARS AWAY!

THE SPACE PROGRAM HAS HELPED PEOPLE IN MANY WAYS. IT HAS LED TO NEW MEDICINES, IMPROVED PRODUCTS, AND NEW WAYS OF GETTING ENERGY. IT HAS UNITED PEOPLE FROM DIFFERENT COUNTRIES. SPACE EXPLORATION IS HELPING US TO UNDERSTAND HOW OUR UNIVERSE—AND PLANET—BEGAN.

OUR JOURNEY INTO SPACE HAS JUST BEGUN. THANKS TO THE BRAVE MEN OF APOLLO 11, AND ASTRONAUTS AFTER THEM, WE CAN TRULY REACH FOR THE STARS!

MORE BOOKS TO READ

The Everything Kids Space Book: All About Rockets, Moon Landing, Mars, and More Plus Space Activities You Can Do at Home! Kathiann M. Kowalski (Adams Media Corporation)

The First Moon Landing. Landmark Events in American History (series). Dale Anderson (World Almanac Library)

The Man Who Went to the Far Side of the Moon: The Story of Apollo 11 Astronaut Michael Collins. Bea Uusma Schyffert (Chronicle Books)

The Moon. Watts Library: Space (series). Margaret W. Carruthers (Franklin Watts)

Space Shuttle: The First 20 Years — The Astronauts' Experiences in Their Own Words. James A. Lovell (DK Publishing)

WEB SITES

Apollo 11
nssdc.gsfc.nasa.gov/planetary/lunar/apollo_11_30th.html

Moon Facts
news.nationalgeographic.com/news/2004/07/0714_040714_moonfacts.html

NASA Kids
kids.msfc.nasa.gov/

Neil Armstrong Air & Space Museum
www.artcom.com/Museums/vs/mr/45895.htm

Please visit our web site at: www.worldalmanaclibrary.com
For a free color catalog describing World Almanac® Library's list of high-quality books and multimedia programs, call 1-800-848-2928 (USA) or 1-800-387-3178 (Canada). World Almanac® Library's fax: (414) 332-3567.

Library of Congress Cataloging-in-Publication Data

Hudson-Goff, Elizabeth.
The first moon Landing / Elizabeth Hudson-Goff and Dale Anderson.
   p. cm. — (Graphic histories)
Includes bibliographical references.
ISBN 0-8368-6203-1 (lib. bdg.)
ISBN 0-8368-6255-4 (softcover)
   1. Project Apollo (U.S.)—Juvenile literature.   2. Space flight to the moon—Juvenile literature. I. Anderson, Dale, 1953- II. Title. III. Series.
TL789.8.U6A535256   2006
629.45'40973—dc22   2005027872

First published in 2006 by
World Almanac® Library
A Member of the WRC Media Family of Companies
330 West Olive Street, Suite 100
Milwaukee, WI 53212 USA

Copyright © 2006 by World Almanac® Library.

Produced by Design Press, a division of the Savannah College of Art and Design
Design: Janice Shay and Maria Angela Rojas
Editing: Kerri O'Hern and Elizabeth Hudson-Goff
Illustration: Layouts by Guus Floor, pencils and inks by Alex Campbell, color by Anthony Spay
World Almanac® Library editorial direction: Mark Sachner and Valerie J. Weber
World Almanac® Library art direction: Tammy West

Printed in the United States of America

1 2 3 4 5 6 7 8 9 10 09 08 07 06